# COMPARING FRACTIONS

## Minta Berry

Crabtree Publishing Company
www.crabtreebooks.com

**Author**: Minta Berry
**Editor**: Reagan Miller
**Proofreader**: Crystal Sikkens
**Cover design**: Margaret Amy Salter
**Editorial director**: Kathy Middleton
**Production coordinator**: Margaret Amy Salter
**Prepress technician**: Margaret Amy Salter
**Print coordinator**: Katherine Berti
**Project manager**: Kirsten Holm, Shivi Sharma (Planman
    Technologies)
**Photo research**: Iti Shrotriya (Planman Technologies)
**Technical art**: Arka Roy Chaudhary (Planman Technologies)

**Photographs:**
Cover: Chris leachman/Shutterstock (girl), Shapiro
Svetlana/Shutterstock (cakes); P5: Monkey Business
Images/Shutterstock; P9: (tl) Argunova/Shutterstock, (tc)
Kzww/Shutterstock, (tr) Kzww/Shutterstock; (ct) Julia
Zakharova/Shutterstock; (cl) Topseller/Shutterstock; (c)
Anelina/Shutterstock, (cr) Anelina/Shutterstock; (bcl) Alexander
Dashewsky/Shutterstock, (bc) Photosync/Shutterstock, (br)
Photosync/Shutterstock; (bl) Denis Tabler/Fotolia; (bc)
Madlen/Shutterstock, (br) Nikola Bilic/Shutterstock; P11:
Kiboka/Shutterstock; P12: (t) EVAfotografie/IStockPhoto, (bl)
EVAfotografie/IStockPhoto, (br) EVAfotografie/IStockPhoto; P17:
(bgd) Leian/Shutterstock; (fgd); Mazzzur/Shutterstock;
Pakhnyushcha/Shutterstock; P18: (t) John Holst/Shutterstock, (b)
John Holst/Shutterstock; P19: (t) Loskutnikov/Shutterstock, (c)
Evikka/Shutterstock, (b) Debbi Smirnoff/IStockPhoto; P20: Jean
Valley/Shutterstock.
(t = top, b = bottom, l = left, c= center, r = right, bkgd =
background, fgd = foreground)

**Library and Archives Canada Cataloguing in Publication**

Berry, Minta
    Comparing fractions / Minta Berry.

(My path to math)
Includes index.
Issued also in electronic formats.
ISBN 978-0-7787-5275-2 (bound).--ISBN 978-0-7787-5264-6 (pbk.)

    1. Fractions--Juvenile literature.
I. Title. II. Series: My path to math

QA117.B465 2011          j513.2'6          C2011-906802-8

**Library of Congress Cataloging-in-Publication Data**

Berry, Minta.
    Comparing fractions / Minta Berry.
       p. cm. -- (My path to math)
    Includes index.
    ISBN 978-0-7787-5275-2 (reinforced library binding : alk. paper) -- ISBN 978-
    0-7787-5264-6 (pbk. : alk. paper) -- ISBN 978-1-4271-8805-2 (electronic pdf) --
    ISBN 978-1-4271-9646-0 (electronic html)
    1. Fractions--Juvenile literature. I. Title.

QA117.B47 2012
513.2'6--dc23

2011040402

# Crabtree Publishing Company

Printed in the U.S.A./112011/JA20111018

www.crabtreebooks.com        1-800-387-7650

**Published in Canada**
**Crabtree Publishing**
616 Welland Ave.
St. Catharines, ON
L2M 5V6

**Published in the United States**
**Crabtree Publishing**
PMB 59051
350 Fifth Avenue, 59th Floor
New York, New York 10118

**Published in the United Kingdom**
**Crabtree Publishing**
Maritime House
Basin Road North, Hove
BN41 1WR

**Published in Australia**
**Crabtree Publishing**
3 Charles Street
Coburg North
VIC 3058

# Contents

# What Is a Fraction?

Mason, Tristan, and Sophie share a pizza. One pizza has eight slices. Each friend wants a different number of slices. Sophie suggests using fractions to solve the pizza problem!

She explains that a **fraction** is a number that describes part of a whole. A fraction is made up of two numbers separated by a line. She draws a pizza and shows that one piece is ⅛ of the whole pizza.

$\frac{1}{8}$

The top number tells how many slices you have.

The bottom number tells how many slices the pizza was cut into.

**Activity Box**

Write the fraction that shows how many pieces were taken.

Fractions show how a whole is divided into parts.

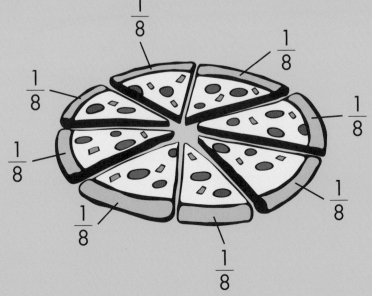

$\frac{1}{8}$ $\frac{1}{8}$ $\frac{1}{8}$ $\frac{1}{8}$ $\frac{1}{8}$ $\frac{1}{8}$ $\frac{1}{8}$ $\frac{1}{8}$

# Numerators and Denominators

Tristan writes the fraction ⅜ on a napkin.
He labels the top number the **numerator**.
He labels the bottom number the **denominator**.

He explains that the numerator 3 shows how many pieces of pizza he wants. The denominator 8 tells how many pieces are in the whole pizza.

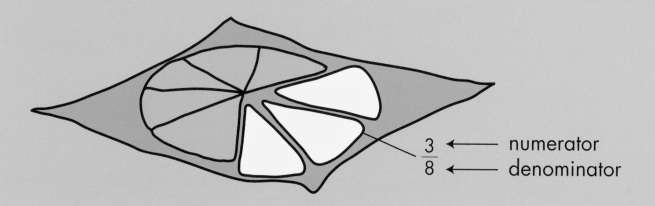

$$\frac{3}{8}$$ ← numerator
← denominator

*To remember that the denominator is the bottom number of a fraction, think "down"-ominator!

| | | |
|---|---|---|
| Tristan wants three pieces of pizza. | $\dfrac{3}{8}$ | |
| Mason wants four pieces of pizza. | $\dfrac{4}{8}$ | |
| Only one piece of pizza is left for Sophie. | $\dfrac{1}{8}$ | |

## Activity Box

A pizza is cut into six pieces. Mason takes two pieces. Write the fraction that shows how many pieces Mason takes.

# Unit Fractions

All fractions that have 1 as the numerator are called **unit fractions**. Unit fractions name one part of the whole. The denominator names the number of parts in the whole.

$$\frac{1}{2} \quad \frac{1}{3} \quad \frac{1}{4} \quad \frac{1}{6} \quad \frac{1}{8}$$

unit fractions

After enjoying the pizza, the friends decide to share an apple. Mason's mom cuts an apple into four equal pieces. Each piece is ¼ of the whole apple.

In a unit fraction, the larger the denominator the smaller the value of the fraction. For example, ¼ of an apple is larger than ⅙ of an apple.

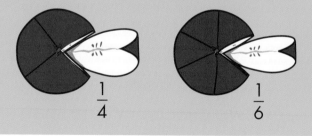

$$\frac{1}{4} \qquad \frac{1}{6}$$

## Activity Box

Name the unit fraction that represents the shaded section in each circle. Put the unit fractions in order from smallest to largest.

*Remember–the unit fraction with the largest denominator has the smallest value.

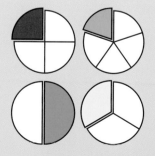

Mason uses vegetables to show unit fractions.

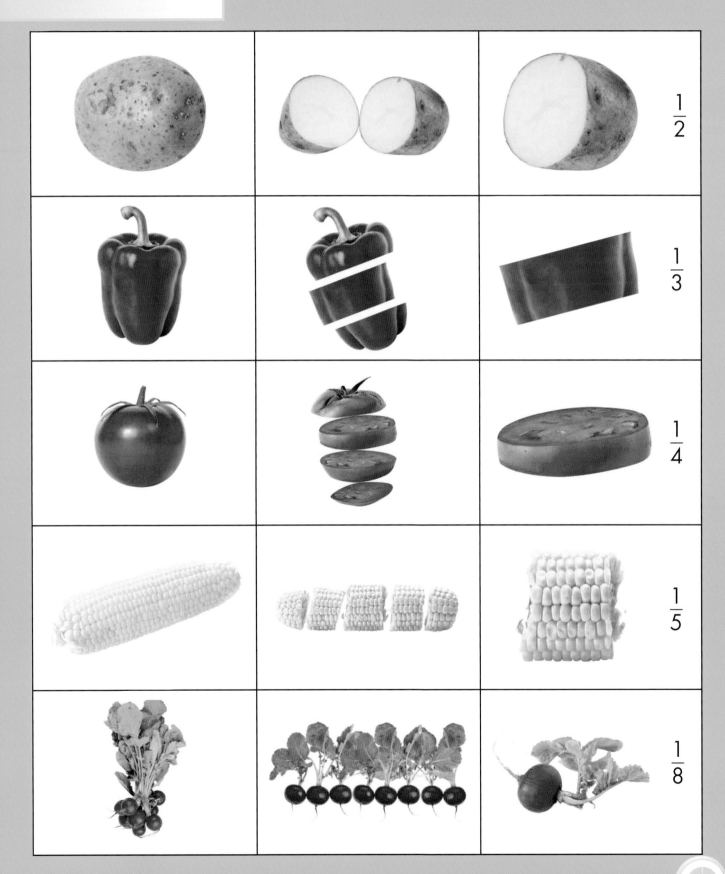

# Fractions on a Number Line

Fractions are parts of a whole. Fractions are numbers that can be compared and ordered. You can compare and order different fractions using a number line.

Mason cuts a potato into two pieces. Each piece represents ½ of the potato. Mason can show this fraction on a number line. Whole numbers are above the line. Fractions are below the line.

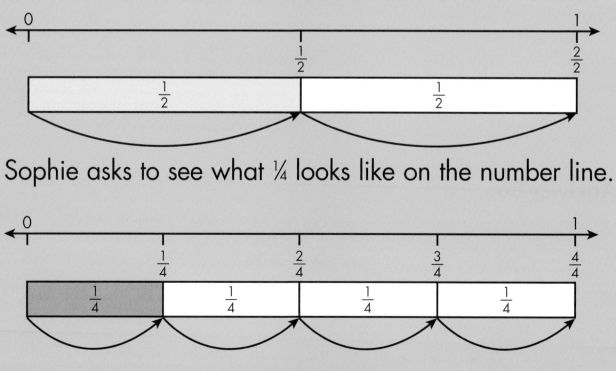

Sophie asks to see what ¼ looks like on the number line.

Sophie sees that ¼ is smaller than ½.

Tristan wants to see more fractions on the number line.

The numerator shows the number of shaded blocks.

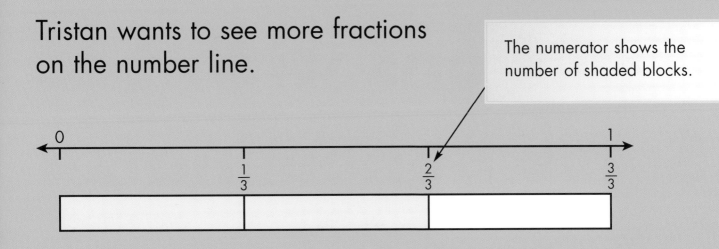

What is the fraction that represents the shaded section of the number line below?

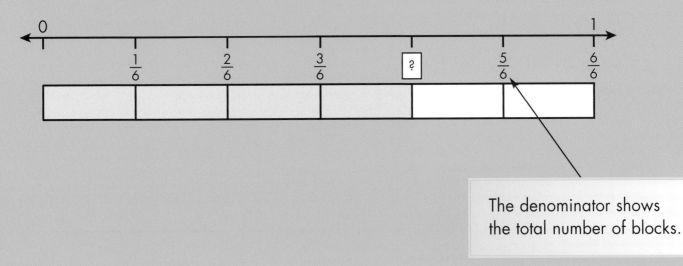

The denominator shows the total number of blocks.

## Activity Box

A chocolate bar is divided into eight squares. Sophie needs six squares to make brownies. Make a number line showing the fraction of the chocolate bar that Sophie needs.

# Fractions with the Same Denominator

While making brownies, Sophie opens a carton of eggs. Sophie uses the eggs to compare fractions with the same denominator. She puts two eggs in one carton. She puts three eggs in another. Each carton holds six eggs.

Which carton has more eggs? Which fraction is bigger? The fraction with the bigger numerator is the bigger fraction.

$\frac{2}{6}$
$\frac{3}{6}$

Each bar has six sections. Six is the denominator of the fractions. The numerator increases as more sections of the bar are shaded. Provide the missing fractions. Which fraction is equal to 1?

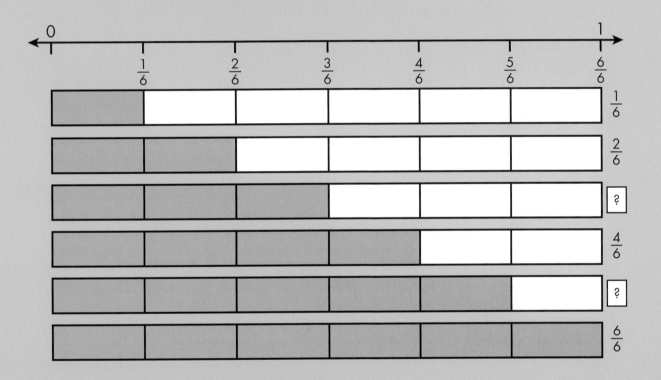

**Activity Box**

Copy the number line on a piece of paper. Place the fractions on the number line in order from smallest to biggest.

$$\frac{5}{8} \quad \frac{2}{8} \quad \frac{6}{8} \quad \frac{1}{8} \quad \frac{3}{8} \quad \frac{8}{8} \quad \frac{4}{8} \quad \frac{7}{8}$$

# Equivalent Fractions

**Equivalent fractions** have the same value even though they look different. They show the same amount in different ways.

Tristan uses waffles to help Mason and Sophie understand equivalent fractions. Tristan shows his friends that ½ is equal to ¼.

Tristan cuts one waffle into two pieces. Each section of waffle is ½ of the waffle.

Tristan cuts another waffle into four pieces. Each section of waffle is ¼ of the waffle. Two sections are ²⁄₄.

Tristan shows his friends that ⁴⁄₆ is equal to ⅔.

Tristan cuts one waffle into six pieces. Each section of waffle is ⅙ of the waffle. Four sections are ⁴⁄₆.

Tristan cuts one waffle into three pieces. Each section of waffle is ⅓ of the waffle. Two sections are ⅔.

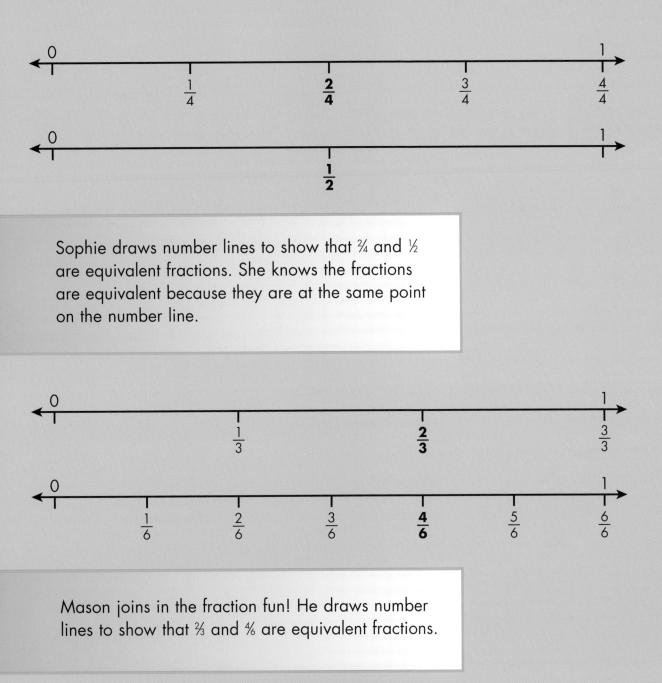

Sophie draws number lines to show that ¾ and ½ are equivalent fractions. She knows the fractions are equivalent because they are at the same point on the number line.

Mason joins in the fraction fun! He draws number lines to show that ⅔ and ⅘ are equivalent fractions.

## Activity Box

Draw four waffles on a piece of paper. Color each waffle to show one of the fractions below. Compare the colored pieces. Are the fractions equivalent?

$\frac{1}{3}$　　　$\frac{4}{8}$　　　$\frac{3}{4}$　　　$\frac{3}{6}$

# Comparing Fractions

Sophie and Mason make a birthday cake. They cut two pieces. One piece is ⅓ of the cake. The other piece is ¼ of the cake.

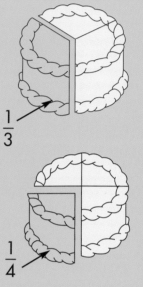

Sophie makes two number lines to show how the pieces compare. It shows that ⅓ of the cake is **greater than** ¼ of the cake.

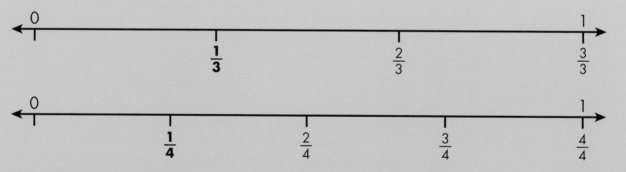

Sophie compares ⅓ of a large cake to ⅓ of a small cake. Each slice is ⅓, but they are not equal. Fractions can only be compared when they are from the same whole.

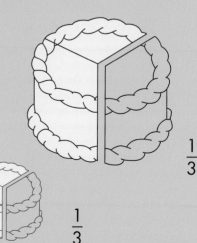

Mason wants to make cupcakes. He needs ¾ cup of flour and ¼ cup of nuts. These fractions have the same denominators. They refer to the same whole (1 cup). The fractions can easily be compared. The fraction that has the greatest numerator is the greatest fraction.

| Ways to Compare Numbers/Quantities | |
| --- | --- |
| Sign | Meaning |
| < | "Less Than" |
| > | "Greater Than" |
| = | "Equal To" |

Mason knows the numerator 3 is greater than the numerator 1. He writes the **number sentence** below to compare the fractions.

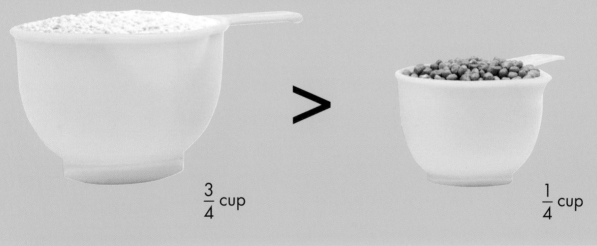

$\frac{3}{4}$ cup     >     $\frac{1}{4}$ cup

## Activity Box

Use >, <, or = to complete each number sentence. You can use the fraction wall on page 23 to help you.

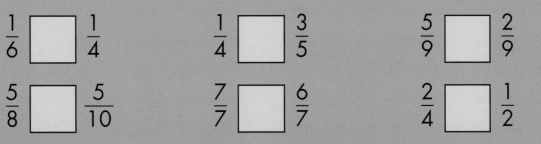

$\frac{1}{6}$ ☐ $\frac{1}{4}$      $\frac{1}{4}$ ☐ $\frac{3}{5}$      $\frac{5}{9}$ ☐ $\frac{2}{9}$

$\frac{5}{8}$ ☐ $\frac{5}{10}$      $\frac{7}{7}$ ☐ $\frac{6}{7}$      $\frac{2}{4}$ ☐ $\frac{1}{2}$

# Whole Numbers as Fractions

A **whole number** is any natural number such as 0, 1, 2, 3, and 4. Tristan writes a whole number as a fraction. He makes the numerator the same number as the denominator.

1 sandwich = $\frac{2}{2}$

One sandwich is cut into 2 pieces. Another is cut into 4 pieces. Tristan writes the whole numbers as fractions.

1 sandwich = $\frac{4}{4}$

### Activity Box

Write each whole number as a fraction.

$1 = \frac{?}{6}$   $1 = \frac{?}{8}$   $1 = \frac{?}{3}$

When the numerator of a fraction is the same as the denominator, the fraction equals 1.

1 apple = $\frac{5}{5}$

1 bag of lemons = $\frac{4}{4}$

1 pie = $\frac{6}{6}$

# Mixed Numbers

**Mixed numbers** are made up of a whole number and a fraction.

Tristan is making trail mix. He measures the ingredients. Then he mixes the raisins, banana chips, apricots, papaya, and other ingredients together.

Now he needs to add 1⅓ cups of cereal. First he measures 1 cup of cereal. Then he measures ⅓ of a cup of cereal.

A mixed number is a whole number plus a fraction.

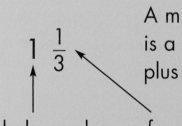

$1\frac{1}{3}$

whole number ⟶ fraction

1          $\frac{1}{3}$ cups

## Activity Box

Write the mixed number for each set of bars.
The first answer is given.

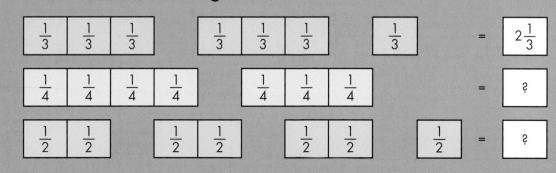

| $\frac{1}{3}$ | $\frac{1}{3}$ | $\frac{1}{3}$ | | $\frac{1}{3}$ | $\frac{1}{3}$ | $\frac{1}{3}$ | | $\frac{1}{3}$ | = | $2\frac{1}{3}$ |

| $\frac{1}{4}$ | $\frac{1}{4}$ | $\frac{1}{4}$ | $\frac{1}{4}$ | | $\frac{1}{4}$ | $\frac{1}{4}$ | $\frac{1}{4}$ | = | ? |

| $\frac{1}{2}$ | $\frac{1}{2}$ | | $\frac{1}{2}$ | $\frac{1}{2}$ | | $\frac{1}{2}$ | $\frac{1}{2}$ | | $\frac{1}{2}$ | = | ? |

When we compare two mixed numbers, we must first compare the whole numbers. If one has a smaller whole number part than the other, then it is the smaller number.

Tristan has 2¼ cups of trail mix in one bag. He has 3⅝ cups of trail mix in another bag. Which is the largest mixed number? Tristan compares the whole numbers. Since 2 is less than 3, he writes the < symbol between the fractions.

$2\frac{1}{4}$ cups < $3\frac{5}{8}$ cups

When the whole numbers are the same, then you need to compare the fraction parts. Tristan has 4¾ cups of trail mix in one bag. He has 4⅓ cups of trail mix in another bag. Which is the largest mixed number? The whole numbers are the same, so Tristan compares the fractions. ¾ is more than ⅓, so he writes the > symbol between the fractions.

$4\frac{3}{4}$ cups > $4\frac{1}{3}$ cups

## Activity Box

Use >, <, or = to complete each number sentence. You can use the fraction wall on page 23 to help you.

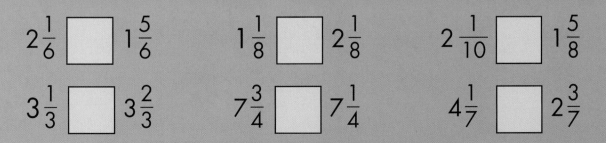

$2\frac{1}{6}$ ☐ $1\frac{5}{6}$     $1\frac{1}{8}$ ☐ $2\frac{1}{8}$     $2\frac{1}{10}$ ☐ $1\frac{5}{8}$

$3\frac{1}{3}$ ☐ $3\frac{2}{3}$     $7\frac{3}{4}$ ☐ $7\frac{1}{4}$     $4\frac{1}{7}$ ☐ $2\frac{3}{7}$

# Glossary

**denominator** The bottom number in a fraction. The denominator names the number of parts in the whole.

**equivalent fractions** Two or more fractions that name the same amount

**fraction** A number that names part of a whole or part of a group

**greater than (>)** A math symbol used to compare two numbers, with the greater number given first

**less than (<)** A fraction smaller than another fraction

**mixed numbers** A number made up of a whole number and a fraction

**number sentence** A math sentence using numbers and symbols (=, –, >, <)

**numerator** The top number in a fraction

**unit fractions** Fractions with a numerator of 1

**whole number** Any natural number such as 0, 1, 2, 3, and 4

$\dfrac{2}{3}$ ← numerator
← denominator

$\dfrac{1}{6}$ ← unit fraction has numerator of 1

$\dfrac{2}{3} = \dfrac{4}{6}$ ← equivalent fractions

$3\,\dfrac{3}{4}$ ← mixed number

## Fraction Wall

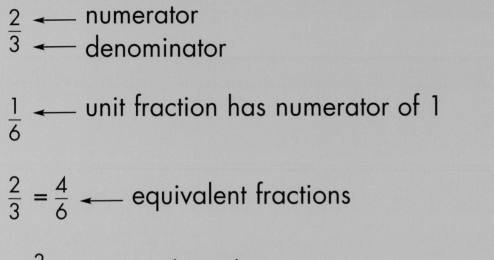

# Index